I0202603

Disappearing Act

Stephen Longfellow

FUTURECYCLE PRESS

www.futurecycle.org

Copyright © 2014 Stephen Longfellow
All Rights Reserved

Published by FutureCycle Press
Hayesville, North Carolina, USA

ISBN 978-1-938853-45-6

*For the women without whom I'd be adrift, especially
my wife Jenny, my sister Elizabeth, and my daughter Rebecca.*

Contents

Change of Command

Far from Home

Cheap digs, this universe:
the day's wallpaper peeled back
—revealing night's—
and the old clerk asleep
among cobwebs of starlight.

The Heart's Wheel

The Question

So, there was a heart, sort of like a canary,
only it had to make a living, and being
no longer needed in the coal mine,
it finally hired on as a bilge pump
for a leaky ship, a bloody bucket,
a real bag of bones. But what else
was the heart to do? Hop down the road
in colorful little pulses, dragging its aorta
in a kind of sad street art of soggy fireworks?
It had tried growing wings, black
as crow, to fly sucking in shadow
and farting out clouds,
but that never got off the ground: a question
of both gravity and light entertainment.
Now it sits in the dark, up to its neck
in warm grease, pumping for its life,
but at least it's doing something.

Disappearing Act

My heart's spent time in all the usual places:

in my mouth, on my sleeve, occasionally
under lock and key, and now on the wall

of a bus-stop kiosk. My heart
remains that shameless, waiting

next to a hastily spray-painted name,
the paint still wet, the spelling suspect,

an alias, I am sure, for someone always
just disappearing around a corner.

Midnight Soliloquy

Alas, my bed's become a scale
knowing nothing but the dead weight
of me, and my head on this white pillow,
a butcher's thumb caught bearing down,
caught making up for a certain lightness.
But I've got company. A shirt-draped chair
is a nearby friend, though I'm sure he's
absentmindedly looking out the window.
And a bit more distantly, the fridge,
a simple god, humming, tidies up
a room for me within its minor universe.

The night's become too much like high school
Latin now—I'm bored, a bit anxious, a little
depressed—lying here, declining the night
away. But the moon outside looks like a quarter
embedded in a ceiling, just out of reach,
part somewhere else among the stars'
smaller change, and the trees
—a thoroughly sorry, wooden lot—stand
with empty arms outstretched,
a chorus of hopeful mourners.

The Heart's Wheel

I might have seen it once
—but what do kids know?—

on the head of a silver pin
at the back of an old woman's drawer

beneath unfinished knitting
for the recent dead, a little lace

and rose petals. There angels

waited, I think, for a lifetime's shift
to end. So long ago.

Oh, patient mice
in your cosmic treadwheel,

do not catch your tails tonight.

Fireplugs

They look so innocent, just standing there
on every corner,

their hard little heads screwed down tight
on stubby shoulders, their mouths

stoppered shut, and their hats
pulled low over their eyes.

They appear harmless little guys,
minding their own business,

but the clouds are out,
there's smoke in the air,

and they're all in touch
through one long, dark root

full of rain.

Startled pigeons break
from a cornice, a fragment

of an old tale. You find yourself
all alone, yet you keep hearing

footsteps on an empty street,
the first drops falling,

and the echoes of sirens
—unlocatable—

but somewhere.

Hagia Sophia, Venice Florida

> Church of the Holy Wisdom...cathedral built at Constantinople
> under the direction of the Byzantine emperor Justinian I. It is a
> unique building and one of the world's great monuments,
> despite time's ravages.
>
> —*Encyclopedia Britannica*

> An American lady who paid ten cents to visit St. Sophia was so
> disappointed that she wanted her money back.
>
> —Herbert J. Mueller, *The Uses of the Past*

In the morning, I awake and, in that lull
before the sleeper grasps exactly who and where
he is, St. Sophie touches the tip of my tongue—

What was I about to say?

Now, on my way to the dentist,
the weatherman tells me what I already know.

And I see her standing
in the doorway of a shuttered souvenir shop, waiting
out the rain, her backdrop an old fresco
of swastikas and names separated
by hearts, a flotsam of food wrappers
awash at her feet, the remnants of offerings.

Or she is the cement-cast Virgin close by
the highway, in an up-ended bathtub, half-buried,
her gaze lowered, arms open, the windows
of the nearby trailer as clouded as the broken eyes
of yesterday's catch. The cars swim
by, old and new and all the same to her.
My little dashboard doggy nods in agreement.

Or she lays me down in her chair, hygienist
with the sad eyes. She sees my every sin, time's
wear on the bone of me: fillings glinting
like veins among a year's worth of slag
and tailings, the pumps working hard

16

and the little miners sweating away night
and day. Clearing the debris, she touches
a nerve but whispers softly in my ear,
forgiving me.

After the storm, I walk along the shore
and collect the fossil shark teeth washed up
from the Gulf, glossy and perfect, among the open
mouths of seashells. A tour boat riffles by
and, masquerading as its figurehead, she looks
resignedly foolish with her jutting breasts and fishtail.

Away, on the horizon, as though in old Byzantium,
beyond the shifting mosaic of light
on nervous water, porphyry columns of rain rise
to the shadowed dome of a thunderhead.

Rural Mailbox

There it stands
before her old Ford Galaxy
with the bench seat pulled out
and propped against a nearby maple.
It's been bruised and battered
by Louisville sluggers,
swung from muddy pickup trucks
and knocked aslant
by January. It waits
at a border of cracked pavement
winding out of sight
through barren fields edged
by scrub and dull barbwire,
past shot-up road signs, broken bottles,
and pools of dirty snow
drifting into summer's dust.
The foreboding haze of something
vague gathers on one horizon,
but the flag is up,
and laid within its rundown universe is
a white envelope filled
with the lilac scent
peculiar to a single memory.
This is the raised fist
whose thumb she'll pull down on
hopefully after
the rain and the mail
have come.

La-Z-Boy

You can bet it enjoys the irony of you
watching *Survivor*, your tired butt sunk
into its lower lip, your sore back slumped
against its upper, and Old Joe,
your big right toe, sticking up in the air,
way out there beyond the footrest.
It loves you too, the slide of your hands
along its duct-taped arms, as you lay them
out, slack-palmed, so wanly you could be falling
asleep during a leisurely transfusion. And
after you crawl off to bed, only Felix, your cat,
will catch the cushions shyly parting
for the delicate tongue that licks the fading
number, penned upon one bandaged arm,
of someone you haven't yet quite forgotten.

Sleeping Dogs

You know it's true. Everywhere dogs lie
chained beneath a chilly infinity of darkness

aflame with grandeur. They wear their sleep
like worn flannel. When they sleep

that's all there is. They dream the world,
lying on their sides, legs running, yips—

where are they? I want to know.

The days of puppyhood I like to imagine,
when the grass was green sun, the nipple

a fountain, and mother a soft hill
to climb and fall asleep upon.

Those dogs were close to the stars then too,
hidden though the stars were

behind a flawless summer sky.

Waste Basket

Furtive little trash can,
I see you
hiding from the bright florescence
of this busy classroom,
under a table, as though beneath
a cedar bent across
a quiet corner
of some forgotten brook.
Your mouth, its delicate flesh
of loose plastic lining, is
like a minnow's—momentary,
motionless, agape—
as though feeding
at a trembling surface
on crumbs from an unseen hand.
Be very still now. There:
the numen of one dark eye
above a great depth. You.

In Passing

You are asleep, Love, as we meet
another big semi so close

it shakes us. And just beyond
the windshield, just out

of sight, just over
the horizon, someone is pulling

this old blue shirt
right off the day's bent back,

trailing behind it
fading scars of jet

vapor, an old barn
collapsing under

the barometer's weight,
a road-cut's clutter of broken

slate and, too far away
to read, another big semi

headed this way. And you are
asleep, Love, so close,

with your face turned away.

But see—just now—
through the window fogged

a little with your breath,
the bright holes the stars begin

to make in the gathered skirts
of the approaching darkness.

Interlude

The shadow on the fence
is my love's. It's a clear day,
and she is working
in our garden. I like watching
the shadow of her happy
to be picking tomatoes this late
in September, yellow leaves
falling, black walnut and silver
maple. The fence I built a year ago
still looks new. The burning
bush is heating up. The air
has no right to be this clear,
her shadow singing
I am here.

Night Court

Film Noir

In Casablanca the shadows
are the real stars. Some

are plants grown larger
than life and as still

as spiders at the edge
of the plot's thin web. Others

are the Oriental forms of
distorted architecture,

behind the evening dresses,
dinner jackets and uniforms.

There are, of course, the countless
shadows of onlooking objects.

The large vase, for example—
fit for a genie—watching

Rick right a wine glass after
a disturbance in the order

of things.

Departure

A moving shadow within the braided canyons of a city
pulls my head up and there, high above,

      moves a multitude
of birds,
    one living purpose,

       wave upon wave,
          in dark, tattered banners

       the wind blows away

    beyond the sheer walls
of concrete and glass

    below the sky's
brilliant river,

       the vertigo
    of movement

    in air
    beneath water,

and I stagger
    as though I
        am standing
still

    as a train pulls away
    from its station,

picks up speed
       —the profound sound
    of its passing—

     my sense

of where I am
            slipping

as I struggle
                    to set myself
        right.

Somewhere Over the Atlantic

Night approaches, and I am alone in my row
as I drink red wine within an unexpected solitude.

    And I know a thing or two, thanks

to the small display embedded in the back of the seat
    before me: that, inches away,

        the air is minus sixty

and that eighty and some odd souls
    in a plane for three hundred plus are

        shooting forward

with one hurricane of a tail wind at
    six hundred and seventy miles per hour

thirty-nine thousand feet above deep, deep water
    somewhere west of Ireland.

    And the engines echo

        like a distant endless avalanche

    while a single light beats

        just for me

at the tip of a slender wing,
    all peach and rose,

within the starry onrushing
    nothing of night

unfolding as a fan in an unseen hand.

The Appointment

A quiet little man sits in a lobby waiting
for a door to open, for someone

to come out, to offer him something—
what doesn't matter—

and because it is a nice day,
the door that he'd already opened,

he'd left ajar. But now

he sees in fragments, frame
upon frame—a red shoe

lifting, gone—a bird's hard eye
piercing, past—within a pram

the head of a child—
and all the time

light insisting
on a shadow

a still life of traffic runs over—
again and again—

and there is no witness—
no, not a hint of

where the body is—skin
after skin, after skin.

Four Dreams of Shadows

The sun hung a shadow
on me and a stranger appeared

at my feet as silent as the moon.
I turned and held my hand

against the sun. My hand glowed
gold laced with rivers of blood.

—

As the prairie flickered
in and out of the wind turbine

blades' eclipsing shadows,
my own shadow wavered

among the long grass
stems like a threadbare suit.

—

There was a still forest,
the leaves as limp, as dark

as sleeping bats. And a voice
said, *Oh you. Oh shadow*

of virtue, your cenotaph
is carried on the backs

of ants and buried
in the garden of your desire.

The moon trembled; the ants
hurried, the earth dragging

at their feet, the water
always rising.

—

It was late but the closet door
was open and in it hung the old,

the misshapen: the sleeves
my arms, the trousers

my legs, the collar, rough,
a hood to pull down

over my face.

—

Blessed is the fork that raises
hand to mouth,

the opulence
of broken glass

after hard rain,
the dreamless sleep

that hides us
from our shadows.

Brick

The brick is the unvarnished mutt
of its family, illegitimate cousin

of stone, the peasant's humble place
of rest behind all the grand marble.

The brick's birthplace is a furnace built
of its self, its midwife is the common

laborer, its birthmark the stain
of the laborer's sweat. The mountain

contains only the mountain and remains
aloofly silent. But the lowly brick

contains a multitude and has a voice
that calls the hand to it.

Public Beach

Across the Gulf's remainders—shell fragments,
empty egg casings, assorted small effluvia
becoming pale sand—long columns of people
weave in and out as ceaselessly restless
as the water's edge: sagging strands of suntan,
fleshy braids suspended between sky and earth,
gravity having its way on a loosely sliding scale
of age and habit and happenstance,
some closer to sand than others; than, say,
the young with bodies as thoughtlessly buoyant
as the large, exotic kites suspended high
in the great pale sky, its thin froth of cloud
spinning out of moment, moving somewhere
else without us, the kites just hovering,
looming like raptors waiting to drop
on a fearful thing that has ventured into the open.

Second Sight

The sun is as white as the snow this morning,
low on the horizon, without heat, chaste.

Her fingers touch the lace
of ice-bound trees, move on,

find their way beyond my eye, deliver
too much careless splendor.

Close relative to infinity—
who can hold onto such a thing?

—

Dust blooms everywhere within a stone mill in December
where stories of open grillwork are powdered

as though with the snow outside. I have climbed
the stair grates upward, my eyes baffled

by a great volume of webbed air, a layered filigree
of steel catwalks and pipes. Here and there

in the unheated space, beasts that eat stone
are hunkered down as though sleeping out

a millennium of winter. Dirty windows filter
translucent gold, a sea of saffron breath

filling a concrete pillow. Near the roof, the mystery
of real feathers lies everywhere

until I see a single pigeon huddled in a corner,
maybe too sick to move, or simply too cold.

—

For divination, then, an eight ball,
a bathysphere in reverse,

and floating out of the fathoms
hoarded in its dark eye,

a bloodless hand waves
against the scratched porthole

—a slow gesture of recognition
in murky water under ice—

then sinks back down into sleep.
Was the answer *Yes* or was it

Concentrate and ask again?

—

On a night train, half-gestures flash
upon my window. Two figures stand together

in the doorway of a tenement, leaning into each other,
talking. Here and gone. I provide them with lives

so I can provide them with names
—Dear Heart, True Love.

Later, above an untamed stillness of branches,
clouds move slowly in the glow of distant cities

like fish stunned by the cold.

Tomorrow

A horse leans against the horizon,
the sky a wall about to fall on him.
In the valley below, little houses
huddle around the glue factory,
stuck together, post and beam,
with the town's one product.
The sky trembles with rain and
the knives point everywhere
but finally enter your heart,
become the gutters running red,
become the street at your feet,
and now the horse descends
slowly in a halo of lightning,
hooves striking thunder.

Yesterday's News

Late night oxygen thief, stillborn wind,
needle without a point, looking for something

else to steal—a beggar's meal, keys
from a blind man's pocket, life and latch

that rattle loosely in the midnight hour, eye
just gone from the locked door's socket,

ragged shadow on the retina's sand,
somewhere on a solitary mote a train cries

for you, for you, you insist, looking up
from the blood-red center of your seed, the cold

stars, their light, all gone, rushing outward. Oh,
I hear you rustling, furtive little mouse

beneath my feet, somewhere under
winter's furnace, within your piss-damp nest

of yesterday's news, the headline reading,
THE WAR WAS WON WITHOUT YOU.

Night Court

Once again there's the extenuating circumstance:

I forgot the heart was loaded.

But, because I never learned Latin, there's nothing to say
in my defense and I am, after all, a serial offender.

The audience, festive riffraff attracted by sordid facts
and sobbing witnesses, know what's up. The gray-haired

lady on the balcony, who looks a little like my mother
and has heard it all before, shakes her head

and returns to her knitting. The judge is plainly a crow
eying the latest road kill. A sleepy jury, no doubt thinking

of an early breakfast, just wants to go home
but they have so many livelihoods to consider first—

the hangman who thoughtfully trims his nails short
and has a way with children, the coroner

with one glass eye who seeks absence, the gravedigger
who knows there's always soil left over for the little garden

that he tends behind the mortuary, the priest
who did learn Latin and reads at the back of the room

rehearsing his lines from a little black book,
the bloodhounds that I've trained myself, who follow a scent

like the Furies and always get their man.

Vaudeville

Vaudeville

Happy to be Hamlet

A dog is barking somewhere
every moment.

            This dog
    —just now—

has nothing urgent about it, is
just a happy soliloquy for whomever

will listen to a knee-high point of view
bounded by a picket fence

about the smell of something
deliciously rotten

out here in the neighborhood.

Appetite

The present is
the guillotine blade

dropped so quickly
we never notice.

—

I fell into a pit of lost keys,
jarring them awake, and they,

like a nest of yellow jackets,
were angry at the buttons

they found in my pockets.

—

Among onions, cabbage, carrots
and one long blonde hair,

a bloodless slab of something
gray steams upon my plate.

The thing in my hand grins—
teeth stainless, shiny and sharp

—and trembles, trembles
like brother tuning fork.

—

Is that a stray gray hair
in my peripheral vision

or the unraveling seam
of her very best dress?

—

Now, whose hand is that,
pushing each instant through

like an endless chain
of sausages?

And who is the customer,
the one testing

with a thick finger
the intestine waiting

next to a bowl of parsley,
the gut like new skin

gleaming

with oil as though
smeared with rainbow?

Mystery

The cat is back after a week-long pilgrimage to
who knows where and sits at the foot of the master's bed

as coolly composed as porcelain. The cat knows
the master must fall asleep in another beer or two,

that the master's mouth will drop open and
the master's soul, which is about the size

and disposition of a mole, will step out humming
an old circus tune to nose and bump about

the room with its clutter of the undiscarded. In one corner
misplaced pictures of friends and family float

within the sea of pages that was a children's volume
of *Kidnapped*—there are the master's parents waving good-bye

to David Balfour! In another corner, on the change-strewn
no-man's-land of a dusty bureau top, a squad of toy soldiers,

rifles pointing everywhere, are holed up behind
soap on a rope, an unfinished letter to a dead father

and a dried-up can of shoe polish. By the window—
that looks out on an old sugar maple, a broken

clothesline and his neighbor's fence—the master's empty
binocular case lies atop issues of *True Detective Stories*

stacked next to a bowl of stale kibble. Enter unseen
demise on silent, furry feet.

The master will rise the next day none the wiser. After all,
there are souls enough waiting in line—each different

but each wearing identical big floppy shoes, baggy pants,
bulbous red nose, fright wig, etcetera—

though not even the cat knows where the line ends.

My Travels with Robert Peary

The Pole at last!!! The prize of 3 centuries, my dream and
ambition for 23 years. Mine at last...

—Robert Peary, his diary, April 7, 1909

Undoubtedly the most driven, possibly the most successful
and probably the most unpleasant man in the annals of polar
exploration.

—Fergus Fleming, *Ninety Degrees North*

In the theater of my head
I'm just a sled dog on his journey.

I've got the desire, if not the heart
without the whip, and frozen herring

isn't exactly an admiralship. Still
I have this idea that if I fought

my way to lead dog, I'd be on top

of the world. In my mind's eye
it would be like being second banana

to a world-class clown
when the show appears

to be just for laughs, but really
the regard of the crowd is all.

—

He is old at 53 in a photo
taken the year he won the prize

of three centuries. His face floats within
a halo of fur, the flesh trails away

from the bleak ridge of his nose,
his cheeks are high

and hollow, his eyes are pebbles
dropped into loose skin,

a large mustache weighs down
his face and appears of a piece

with the ruff of his hood, his mouth
is hidden in shadow—that is all

to be seen of Robert Edwin Peary.
Still, try to imagine a few

painted tears, a pair of baggy pants,
big floppy shoes—not to mention

me with my perky ears just outside
the camera's field of view.

—

In my armchair I am
with you just now, Sir.

And I say, *Monkey see.*
Monkey do! Take a snapshot,

someone please,
of my spectral tail,

my prehensile presumption,
my swinging I

caught in mid-
somersault.

—

Offstage, out there
in all that cold white,

what was left
with the layers peeled

away? Down
of the goose, fur

of the wolf, fleece
of the sheep, silk

of the worm, buttons
of bone, perhaps

the self just
a glittering ribbon

of breath
streaming away.

Ode to a Feeling

that I am, just now, a boiled potato
happy to be sitting on fine china,

a perfectly peeled spud upon a plain
of equally dazzling brilliance.

I used to have eyes, but
I mislaid them somewhere...

However, residing as I do forever
in this moment, I have to ask,

Who really needs them?

It's enough to know
my world is white and round,

much like myself, the sun

fixed in its place, and infinity
a cozy glow fading away

beyond the horizon. I'd punch
the air (if I had a hand)—*Yes!*

—for this must be akin
to what the first potato felt

in its Eden, a tuber freshly risen
up under the foot of a ruminant

who had just begun to consider
a feeling of its very own

yet to be named *Hunger.*

—

I have a feeling I've been here
before, sliced in half but not missing

the part I left behind. The knife
was a sharp one, its touch

like warm butter, and I'd recall
old Occam's razor except

I've already forgotten. Ah, but
a tongue awaits, old boat rocking

in a canal that stretches from here...
to porcelain.

Now, balanced on an edge
and lifted up, the moment invites me

to tell it my name but, alas,
I don't remember.

No Place Like Home

In the middle of the night our houses suddenly lifted themselves
up on the long legs we never knew they had and moved
out from our coziest imaginings onto our horizons.
Some of us were tumbled out of doors or windows and fell
to our deaths while others jumped in sheer terror. Still others
were crushed by the fall and slide of large pieces
of furniture. The rest of us simply held on, until this unthinkable
thing sorted itself out and we could move to our windows
to see what was happening. What we saw in the light of a full moon
was messy: restless homes trailing the remains
of their infrastructure—rat tails of wiring and plumbing—
as well as the odd willow whose roots had grown too much
into a foundation or a patio flapping along
like the open rear-panel of a union suit.

Still, the houses were oddly beautiful and surprisingly quick
for their size, scuttling along like Godzilla-sized crabs
on dainty legs. At first they seemed a bit dazed and unsure
of exactly which way to go as they milled around
and jostled each other. Unmindful, maybe, but imagining
something—for they soon sorted themselves out and began following
the streets in one direction, leaving their neighborhoods behind
as they smoothly merged, zipper-fashion, at all the intersections.
In a way it was democratic progress, the big mansions,
middle-class tracts, and rundown tenements
all cooperating in the gathering march.

The National Guard got out the big guns
but there were people aboard most of the houses and it was hard
bringing one down anyway. No one could figure out what was head
and what was ass and a house on the move only stopped
when it was a quivering pile of bite-sized rubble. There were just
too many, no time to make a plan, and, in the end—on board or off—
all we could do was watch as they followed the highways
in long columns headed for the sea where those still on board
at last jumped out before their beloved shelters vanished underwater.

Why I am Never Lonely

No matter where I am, the knife and fork are there
to keep me company. More than familiar,

they are family. My hands are only clubs
without them. Thus when I grasp the knife and fork

and the faces of my thumbs look up at me expectantly,

I feel the strength of the earth's deep waters rise
through the upward thrusting stem of my hunger

and into my clenched hands. The earth sings,
Red! The earth sings, *Bloody!* It's such a happy party!

And the meal—the quotidian cut up short, arranged
as tiny fingers pointing everywhere; a bowl of the oracular,

stewed to sky-blue blindness; three amusing monkeys,
stuffed, hands placed in the traditional manner over

the mouth, the eyes and the ears. When I am done,
I don't just lick my fingers clean and leave

the knife and the fork behind as though
they were strangers at someone else's table—no—

I tuck them quietly away next to my heart
where they sleep until the next time.

Four Evening Theatricals

Each day the trees weave the sky
her darkness. Under their branches—

when I am there—sometimes the light
captures my eye, sometimes I walk

within the unfolding pattern
and feel a little bereft when the trees

stow their shuttles away. But then—
sometimes—I notice the sky

wrap the sequined night about her
and begin her journey toward morning.

—

Just now—from the bottom—
the world is a saucer of air

held by a Las Vegas Elvis
who cradles the rim

with mascara-stained fingers
and croons to whomever will listen

as a distracted moon looks
for a place to put down her teacup.

—

This evening is a car-wreck
of oranges—all shredded rind,

pooled opalescence
and skid marks. And the stars

are already arriving
at the scene with their starry

preoccupation, a gathering
of bored luminaries all dressed

pretty much the same. A dog
begins to sing the blues,

lays out its guileless longing
slowly on the still evening air.

It takes a dog to be truly
impressed, which is to say

truly humble—how it raises
its muzzle to the evening

and sings without expectation
for the ruins of a day.

—

The dog is walking
me this winter evening

and it is cold but I stop

to listen for no reason
except that I

just noticed the day
looking over her shoulder

at me, her improbable arms
spread across the sky

as though they were
sunset, as though,

before she drew
closed her curtains,

she had one last,
important

thing to say.

Archeology

What is meant by reality. It would seem to be something
very erratic, very undependable—now to be found in a dusty
road, now...

—Virginia Woolf, *A Room of One's Own*

                                Its dusty tines point away
            from me. One spears a forest

        as though the trees
                were broccoli; the other bends
down into

a valley's mouth.
        Where my impatient feet

                    have shuffled
                    in the dusty road,
        wanting to know
        just whose fork this is,
a bit of silver

            begins to show,
                    begins to reveal

        a pale reflection.

Three Whistles for a Graveyard

Brahms claimed to hear the giant
footsteps of Beethoven always

behind him, though I suspect
what really registered

on his mind was the shadow
of the soul descending.

—

You've just knocked over Plato's cave
and there's a stain on the floor

like flowing shadow,
but you don't care

because the mug is lying
propped on its chipped handle

and you're down on your knees
with your ear to its mouth,

very certain you hear
little voices.

—

The old cleaning woman, calling it
a night, leaves behind

a single bruised thumbnail
on the brightening wall of the sky.

And the worn gray floor
of the lake looks polished too, under

the ragged coattails of a great crowd
of fog wisps who couldn't care less

as they jostle along
toward the closing doors of darkness.

Vaudeville

Oh, one-legged man,
your suspenders

clasp you like hands
holding the world up

and you lean into them

as into a stiff wind or
as a horse in a harness

would, pushing forward
one step at a time.

—

Oh, one-legged man, your arms
are strong and carry you into

the tree tops where the leaves
sweetly clap. Now

you're out on a limb
and float in the sky

as day floats into night
like a salmon returned home

and quietly decomposing.

—

Oh, one-legged man, playing
at pirate, a dough hook hangs

from your cuff like a question-
mark asking what you have left

up your sleeve. Long John,
the kids love you at parties.

Arghh! You say... *Arghh!*
as you lift the patch from your eye

and wink at the little one
who clings to your crutch

because life is still just
a balancing act.... *Arghh!*

—

Oh, one-legged man, looking
at an old photograph

hung in an antique frame,
your reflection floats there

on the glass and reminds you
of an anamorphosis,

the oddly distorted skull
painted by some old master

who might have known
what he was doing.

—

Oh, one-legged man, your sock
fits like a glove on your hand

and reminds you of childhood,
reminds you of Lamb Chop.

So, what do you say, Mr. Sock?
Shaped like Italy.

Of course.
And ears like an elephant.

Impossible. No ears at all.
No? But, I see their great lobes

at my sides, wiggling
like toes, oh, one-legged man.

The sock sways before you
with a life of its own,

a faceless trunk searching
with a keen sense of smell

and, suddenly afraid
of the least misstep,

you freeze. Then you laugh,
putting it away in a box

of loss for the last footstep
abandoned.

—

Oh, one-legged man, alone
in your room, watching

your step in a glass half full
with left-right irony, you laugh.

But you were once
quite a dancer, and your pants,

like a vaudeville's drawn curtains,
reveal one shoe still listening

for the last of the applause.

Change of Command

Communion

After all these years, it's as though
you are a long-lost friend.

Sit down.

I have something I want to tell you
and this moment may not come again

for today I am a living heart
laid out upon a table set for anyone.

Sit down.

Pretend the silverware and crystal
have been polished just for you,

pretend the linen is unstained
and the plate, the best bone china.

For this is an occasion.

Notice the waiter
pulling out a chair for you.

The look he has reminds me
of our father; the look says,

Eat what I have placed before you.

Better sit now
and, besides, you are very hungry,

and I,

I am still beating.

Ghosts

This morning there is the mirror and the face
before I shave.

       Hello, Face,
I say.
       You're looking well

—a harmless lie as I play for time—

but the feeling rises in the hand that holds
the razor, a feeling like when I was

a child and the night

brushed its stiff beard against my curtained window
or, a few years later, when I was newly grown,

a volunteer fireman,

and around my ankles the smoke
rising from a black stubble of burned grass

drifted momentarily
in nervous little wisps

that were like hands
that wanted pockets—

fearful little hands
the wind carried away

into a blue sky
without a cloud in sight.

Postcard to a Brother

The clouds know which way the wind is blowing, trailing the days
behind them like fish strung together, gill to gill. They have the drift
of bored fishermen calling to each other:

> *This is not the place.*

We are broken anchors, you and I, long ago cut loose, apart,
half-buried, as the unknown continents of shadows
sweep toward us, eclipse us, and leave us in their wake.

But it is the daylight, really, that gives us the chills,
that makes us button up and go inside.

Down the street, the mailman pauses to pick his teeth
and scratch his ass as he ponders a name he ought to know
in front of the house whose curtains are always drawn,
the house from which comes not even the slightest whimper.

I send you this from far away and I say,

> *The clouds are a mystery to me here.*

I have not kept track of a single one,
not even the first, the one in the shape of our mother,
the one that suggested things would be okay.

Small Bites of Winter

Twenty below, and tulips unfolded
for such sun flowing through glass

as though tulips were all.
—

On the snow, the notion of trees
rested in blue shadow.
—

I found absence on a lake:
an island whose snow showed

no footsteps.
—

Where the ice was restless
against the shore, a pool

of blackest water,

and within, much darker still,
the numinous eye of an otter.
—

Snow on bare branches buried
the shadows

until the wind
set them free.
—

The pine bowed, burdened
with snow, but for one green branch

floating in the sunlight.
—

On a still morning when air
had no more substance than the spaces

between the stars, night's last breath
was a blue mist that lingered

upon the lake's white breast.

The Wind in the Leaves

The autumn wind is the clearing
of a brittle throat,
like my mother's voice
after she'd tucked me away
on a quiet night between
clean white sheets,
then shushed away the cat
at my feet with a sound
that was more of a rattle
than either of us wanted.

Lost

The witch's house must have appeared
this way to Hansel: as bright as a lantern

within a fist of trees, their shadows
leaking out between clenched fingers,

and next to it an open vein of water,
water like broken glass the evening

has cut her finger on. *Oh Sister,*
let us hurry to that one thing,

to that one shining thing with smoke
floating above it like a thin gray shroud.

Fist with a Thumb in It

Raised before you, it is the totem,
the distant ancestor with a low brow
and a bony crest. With thumb tucked in,
it makes a grim mouth, its jaw thrust out,
and at first you think it has no eyes
but, looking closely, you see the eyes
are empty lids sewn shut. Around
the thumb, the fingers curve tightly
inward, their faces buried deep
in the floor of your palm...

—

Before the tongue, there came the thumb
to make its statement, to stand
in opposition to what had always been.

Follow me,

it told the rest of the fingers.

*We will become God's
chosen tool and our tribe will prosper.
We will craft a glorious jewel and call
it the City. And, because the world
around us is cruel and is not God's
Hand, we will make a fist to beat it down.*

—

Maybe you learn to make a fist
from your father. You are a little boy
who likes to talk and this makes you
his sore thumb. He lays his hammer
down and you see his clever hand
raised high and strong and open
against the light of a window.

The hand plummets out of the light
as your own hand curls shut
on its own. You have made a little fist
and you learn to put it in your mouth.

—

A hot anger has plummeted into the face
of the City, and you are Now. You are
the fist within the iron glove, the bee
within the iron throat, the deep
diesel drumming, siren wail, AIR HORN.
You are the relentless wheel
and the flex of steel holding the dark
pond's surge pressing in your gut.
And you think you are bearing down
—finally bearing down—
on something that's always been waiting
just around the corner
just for you.

—

I apologize for being
an awkward fist, its thumb
tucked in and good
for nothing but hurting itself.

Familiar Space

Uneasy stranger that I am in this lifelong blind date
with myself, the mirror reassures me

that I take up a small amount of familiar space.

I turn and, yes, the iron bed is still there
with soft pillows, cold white sheets,

a comforter, and the lamp beneath
whose parchment shade I lay

my glasses before I close my eyes.
And beyond that there's

the blank wall of oblivion—

when it is not an ear
pressed against the world,

an ear to hear
what the wind has woken:

the infinity of leaves, the clamor
of distant trains, misfortune's sirens

speeding somewhere, the sudden axe
of drunk and unreasoned laughter,

and sometimes in an unexpected silence, a tiny creature
caught by something larger than itself.

I return my eyes to the mirror
and see myself standing within

a rising mist of tarnished silver
and a minor blemish easily missed,

a scratch like faint lightning
running through me from shoulder to hip

before vanishing off the mirror's edge.

Dog As Antonym

It's early morning and again I wake to the lingering
echo of footsteps although the black Lab that lies
next to me sleeps on ever so soundly without a woof.
Sam is nothing like those half-crazy dogs who bark
all day with their hackles up at hints of shadow
just around corners. These self-histories
we humans carry in our too-large heads create
a context for us to see the future, but those poor dogs—
in the now forever—are as sure of some phantom presence
as I am sure of nothing.

Sunrise

The morning touches
a cut lip,

remembers what

dreams the night
had brought

to mind. Stand by

this window with me;
see how the sky

holds no grudge, holds

nothing of its own,
finding her way here

one more time,
empty hands open.

Junkyard

In a summer evening's warm humidity
predators feed among the old cars, parts
everywhere like stained vertebrae, like broken
ribs and battered skulls, like bleached hoof and torn claw.
After the rain, the cats lounge, languorous,
across scabrous hoods, above oil-laced puddles
full of the fractured glass of a fading hour
shot through with slow fire. A sagging bench seat,
partially disemboweled, vinyl hide curling,
lies like the survivor of some lost gulag
finding release in a happenstance of light.
It offers still a certain under-stuffed comfort
for an old, scarred tabby with one closed eye
watching the shadows for its next small meal.

A Little Bit of Silence

A little bit of silence dares me to try
to fill it with something it doesn't
already know.

A ceiling fan hangs above me waiting
for summer, or maybe suspended
like some spread-eagled cartoon character
who, having skidded out beyond cliff's edge,
waits now for the ground, taking its own
sweet time deciding just when to rush upward.

Yes, says the green silence, *see its body,*
wide open for the embrace, grow
heavy with regret...and how
the moving shadow of a branch outside
the window is an old phonograph arm
stuck on one scarred fragment of
                              a love song.

Little Prayers to St. Sisyphus

Pray for us who have
wheels beyond counting,

who have wheels enough
to make you cry.

—

Bringer of hope
in your eternal task,

we remember:
you cheated death twice

and lived to old age
despite a god's anger.

—

Patron saint
of the sine wave,

of rhythm
and period,

of dancing
and circles,

you, who turns up smiling
balanced on your bicycle

in our midnight games
of solitaire,

remember us.

—

To the crazy lady under
the overpass,

who each evening pushes
her shopping cart

up to a drum of fire
and sings, sweet Sisyphus,

to her we offer up
our change.

Philosopher's Stone Café

It's always late here, but
I'm surprised anyway

that it's so crowded where
I'd thought I might be alone

except for the guy who makes
the coffee and fills the cups.

The coffee is good here,
like living stone,

polished and black.

When I enter,
everyone looks up

without recognition
before returning

to their cups, which
contain small amounts

of night each stirs absent-
mindedly with a spoon.

Afterthought

I can imagine the world without
me, absence moving in

to take up residence, leaving
the small curiosa of my life

where I had forgotten them,
befriending the dust

and cobwebs, feeding
the crumbs of the unfinished

to her sleek, gray mice,

sitting with folded hands
by an open window waiting

for the spring rain to come.

Change of Command

All goes onward and outward, nothing collapses,
And to die is different from what any one supposed, and luckier.

—Walt Whitman, "Song of Myself"

There you are again, the sun's hand
on your shoulder, your hands clasped behind
you in obsequious patience, the scent
of clipped grass, the air intimate
with your ear, chin up, eyes straight,
hidden within the long, still ranks,
beyond the shade of a viewing stand
full of anonymous importance,
witness to another coming
and going with the beating of drums
and a good brass band all done up
in ribbons, the sweet blue sky
an opening iris leading you out
into the garden of an infinite
silence. Beyond the buzzing
of another day's words,
there is nothing for you,
standing there waiting, except chance
and the universe brushing against your
skin, the random motion of now
miraculously arranging into
a line of iridescent clouds rising
from behind the horizon, and a vision
occurs to you: that it is you
who is moving, cold and high,
and that beyond, in the hidden darkness,
lie the ruins of a forever you cannot
comprehend, a vastness of quartz dust
scattered wide under the heel of a boot,
maybe a big dipper promising water enough
as, gratefully, you fall asleep.

Acknowledgments

Café Review: "Rural Mailbox"
Crannóg: "Why I am Never Lonely"
Diner: "The Question," "Fire Plugs," "Fist with a Thumb in It"
Foundling Review: "Postcard to a Brother"
A Hudson View Poetry Digest: "Dog as Antonym"
In Posse Review: "Ghosts," "Vaudeville"
Literary House Review: "Communion," "The Heart's Wheel"
The Literary Review: "Little Prayers for St. Sisyphus," "Second Sight"
Los Angeles Review: "Junkyard"
OVS Magazine: "Sunrise"
The Pedestal: "Mystery"
Pif: "Change of Command"
Prick of The Spindle: "A little bit of silence…," "No Place Like Home"
Prism: "Midnight Soliloquy"
Quiddity: "Departure," "In Passing"
Rhino: "Lost"
Spillway: "Night Court"
Summerset Review: "Wastebasket," "Small Bites of Winter"
Sweet: "Hagia Sophia, Venice, Florida," "Interlude"
Talking River Review: "Far from Home"
Underground Voices: "The Appointment"
Word Riot: "Happy to be Hamlet"

I am grateful to the Southeast Minnesota Arts Council (SEMAC) for the Opportunity Grant that helped complete the final revision of this collection.

Cover art, "Sun behind leafs," by jubr; author photo by Solan Sadoway; cover and interior book design by Diane Kistner (dkistner@futurecycle.org); Gentium Book Basic text with Expletus Sans titling

About FutureCycle Press

FutureCycle Press is dedicated to publishing lasting English-language poetry books, chapbooks, and anthologies in both print-on-demand and ebook formats. Founded in 2007 by long-time independent editor/publishers and partners Diane Kistner and Robert S. King, the press incorporated as a nonprofit in 2012. A number of our editors are distinguished poets and writers in their own right, and we have been actively involved in the small press movement going back to the early seventies.

The FutureCycle Poetry Book Prize and honorarium is awarded annually for the best full-length volume of poetry we publish in a calendar year. Introduced in 2013, our Good Works projects are devoted to issues of universal significance, with all proceeds donated to a related worthy cause. Our Selected Poems series highlights contemporary poets with a substantial body of work to their credit.

We are dedicated to giving all of the authors we publish the care their work deserves, making our catalog of titles the most diverse and distinguished it can be, and paying forward any earnings to fund more great books.

We've learned a few things about independent publishing over the years. We've also evolved a unique, resilient publishing model that allows us to focus mainly on vetting and preserving for posterity the most books of exceptional quality without becoming overwhelmed with bookkeeping and mailing, fundraising activities, or taxing editorial and production "bubbles." To find out more about what we are doing, come see us at www.futurecycle.org.

www.ingramcontent.com/pod-product-compliance
Lightning Source LLC
Chambersburg PA
CBHW070008100426
42741CB00012B/3152

* 9 7 8 1 9 3 8 8 5 3 4 5 6 *